CW00863189

Leaves from
the Tree of Heaven

Leaves from
the Tree of Heaven

Reflections on Prayer

AUGUSTINE HOEY Ob.OSB

Note for Librarians: A cataloguing record for this book is available from Library and Archives
Canada at www.collectionscanada.ca/amicus/index-e.html
ISBN 1-4251-1069-X

Unless otherwise stated, this Scripture quotations
in this publication are taken from The Jerusalem Bible
copyright 1966, 1967 and 1968 By Darton, Longman & Todd
Ltd and Doubleday & Co. Inc.

Original design by Sandie Boccacci.
Intype, London Ltd.

Offices in Canada, USA, Ireland and UK

Book sales for North America and international:
Trafford Publishing, 6E–2333 Government St.,
Victoria, BC V8T 4P4 CANADA
phone 250 383 6864 (toll-free 1 888 232 4444)
fax 250 383 6804; email to orders@trafford.com
Book sales in Europe:
Trafford Publishing (UK) Limited, 9 Park End Street, 2nd Floor
Oxford, UK OX1 1HH UNITED KINGDOM
phone 44 (0)1865 722 113 (local rate 0845 230 9601)
facsimile 44 (0)1865 722 868; info.uk@trafford.com
Order online at:
trafford.com/06-2828

10 9 8 7 6 5 4 3 2 1

For Cardinal Basil Hume OSB
who has been to me a Father
in God.

Contents

Foreword

As we move into the next millennium we must become, increasingly, persons of prayer. Many people want to. Prayer puts us in contact with God, or, more accurately allows Him to enter into our lives. That is important.

Prayer demands effort. Few of us pray naturally. We have to learn how to pray, practise it, keep at it.

Father Hoey has given us a book that will help beginners to get started, and indeed will give encouragement to those who need it. We all do.

Father Hoey has had long experience as a spiritual director. He speaks with authority.

Basil Hume.

Introduction

We do not learn to cook by reading cookery books. We do not learn to pray by reading books on prayer, but they can be a support to our practice.

Prayer is about a personal relationship with God and our neighbour. *God, the Holy Spirit, is the teacher of prayer.*

We only learn to pray by praying
and by praying again
and by praying again
and *never giving up*.

We pray as we can and not as the books say we ought.

Each of us is a unique creation of God and so no two people relate in exactly the same way to God.

The following pages are reflections on what seems real to me after many years of trying to pray. Most of them will seem obvious. I am grateful to the many writers of books and articles on the subject of prayer and spirituality which I have read. Their thinking has unconsciously influenced mine. Nothing new can be written on the subject of prayer.

Augustine Hoey Ob.OSB

1

Silence and Darkness
Listening to God

There was silence in heaven for about half an hour.
(Rev. 8:1)

We are all familiar with the story of Samuel listening to God (1 Sam. 3:1–14). Samuel was a server in the Temple at Shiloh, working under the priest Eli. It was part of his job to sleep in the Temple at night for security reasons. One night, after locking up, Samuel was lying on his mattress in the silence and the darkness of the empty Temple, when he heard his name being called, 'Samuel, Samuel'. He thought it must be Eli wanting something. He went to Eli, who said, 'No. I didn't call you. Go back to sleep.' This happened three times. On the last occasion Eli said, 'Well now, if you hear the call again, reply and say, "Speak, Lord. Your servant is listening."' Samuel went back and lay down in the silence and the darkness. Just as he was falling asleep he heard the voice again. He responded and God spoke to him, asking him to do something which was very difficult. He had to go and tell Eli that Eli and all his family were going to be destroyed.

This story of Samuel is relevant for us in the following interesting ways. It was in the darkness and the silence of the night that God spoke. At first, it never crossed Samuel's mind that it could be God speaking. He had to discuss the matter with a priest. He needed help to realise it was not just his imagination before he could respond to God.

Silence. The silence of the night in the Temple.

Silence today is not very fashionable. We live in an increasingly noisy world. In the city there is the constant roar of traffic on the roads and in the air. But we also have to suffer other noise. It is called 'background music' and there is no escape from it. This background noise bombards us in the super-market, in restaurants, cafés, some railway stations, in aeroplanes and on the telephone while waiting for a call to be transferred. In many public houses and other venues the music is so amplified, so over-powering, that no kind of verbal communication is possible. Why do we need this background noise? What is it for? No one is listening to it. How many of us, the minute we enter our homes, switch on something which will make a noise – a stereo, the radio, the television – not because we are going to listen to it or even watch it. Why do we need this? For many it is compulsive. Is it because in silence we are brought face to face with ourselves and we don't like that. We don't like looking inside our-selves. Uncomfortable questions surge to the surface, 'What is my life all about? Where am I going? Who cares anyway?'

There is no knowledge of God without silence. It may seem paradoxical to say silence is the sound of God! Yet this great truth is made clear over and over again in the Bible, in the life of Our Lord and in the lives of the saints. 'Be still and know that I am God' (Ps. 46:10, RSV).

Remember Moses (Exod. 3:1–12). When did he discover what God was asking him to do? It was not when he was having discussion groups with people about it. It was when he was in the wilderness which is always the place of silence. There in the silence he had that profound experience of God which he described as a burning bush. He heard God speaking to him and telling him what he had to do. As with Samuel it was something very difficult – in fact on the surface well nigh impossible. He was to go and free his own Jewish people from their Egyptian slavery.

It was the same with Elijah (1 Kings 19:9–18). Elijah was a bit like us. He was, as it were, on the side of God, and he found, as we do in today's world, that it is not a very popular occupation. People do not like our Christian views and opinions. Elijah had made his views so clear that he was in danger of being arrested and killed. So, he ran away, and where did he go? He went up into the mountains into the place of silence, into a cave which again speaks of silence and darkness. He wanted God to do something which would compel belief. He thought that, if only God would do something spectacular and terrifying, people would be shocked into believing. We read, 'There came a mighty wind, so strong it tore the mountains and shattered the rocks. But God was not in the wind. After the wind came an earthquake. But God was not in the earthquake. After the earthquake came a fire. But God was not in the fire.' Each time Elijah thought, 'this is it'. God is going to speak. Yet, it was only after all the noise and confusion had died away that Elijah in the darkness and silence of his cave heard a whisper, like a very gentle breeze. It was the voice of God. Elijah threw his cloak over his face and fell to the ground in awe and wonder.

It is in darkness and silence that God makes his will clear to us. Consider how the great things God has done for us in Christ (the saving acts of redemption) were carried out under conditions of darkness and silence. We usually associate activity with noise. But God doesn't work that way. So, when, in his great love and concern for us, he decided to become one of us, under what conditions did that great activity of God take place? God placed his seed in the womb of Mary in absolute silence. In the darkness of the womb God's Son began to grow and nobody knew anything about it except Our Lady Mary and later, Joseph.

It was just the same when it came to the moment of physical birth. It did not take place in the crowded inn amidst the noise and bustle of those staying there. It took place in the silence of the stable and in the dark. 'When all things were in quiet silence and night in the midst of her swift course thy almighty Word leaped down from Heaven' (Wisdom 18:14).

And when we come to the end of Our Lord's life, the moment when he made the final choice for death and took upon himself the sins of all the world, under what conditions did this mighty act of God take place? It was after the Last Supper, and Jesus and his friends had left the noise and chatter of the Passover pilgrims in the streets of Jerusalem. They went outside the city walls to the Garden of Gethsemane, to a place of silence in the darkness of the night. There, our Lord, all alone because the friends he had taken with him had fallen asleep, accepted the burden of the sins of the world. Who can plumb the depths of such a mystery? He, the sinless one, took on himself all the sins of the human race, past, present and to come. It was an intolerable burden. Our Lord was in anguish and distress; again and again he cried out for the burden to be removed. Outwardly there was nothing to show that the world's salvation was at stake. In the silence of the garden and the darkness of the night the final acceptance of God's plan for our redemption was made.

It is the same at the crucifixion. We are told that a darkness came down around the cross – a darkness which in the midday of the blazing Palestinian sun would bring its own uncanny sense of silence and awe. Our salvation was being wrought in darkness and silence.

When God did for us the greatest thing he has ever done – the event on which the whole of Christianity is based – when he raised up Jesus from the dead, under what conditions did this mighty activity of God take place? It was in the darkness before the dawn, and the hour before the dawn is always the most silent part of the night. In silence and in darkness Christ rose from the dead.

Throughout his earthly life Our Lord was always trying to show us how necessary silence and darkness are for us, if we are ever going to relate closely to him and discover God's will for our lives. When, after his baptism, he began to prepare for his own public life, where did he go? Jesus chose the wilderness, the place of silence. There, all alone, and in the silence of the day and the long darkness of the night, wrestling with the Devil's suggestions to take short cuts, he planned his public career.

During the long crowded days of his public ministry, when his ears and those of his disciples were constantly ringing with the cries and demands of the crowds, 'Lord, save me', 'Lord, help me', 'Lord, that I may receive my sight', 'Lord, the one you love is sick', what did Our Lord say to the disciples when they were utterly worn out and emotionally exhausted? 'We've done enough. We must leave them now. We haven't finished but they will still be here when we come back. We must get our priorities right. We must go away into a desert place and rest' (Mark 6:31). The desert is the place of silence and listening. Active work for God will bear no fruit unless it springs from silence and stillness.

Time after time, we are told in the Gospels, Our Lord would leave everyone and go into the desert, into the hills, climb the mountains or cross the lake of Galilee, in order to find silence, to enter into that unity which is his with the Father and the Holy Spirit. He often spent the whole night in prayer on the hills. It was on such an occasion, in the darkness of a night in prayer, that he made his decision as to whom to choose for his twelve apostles (Luke 6:12–16). And when he was teaching us about prayer, he told us to go into a room alone and close the door, shutting other people out. This is just another way of telling us to go into a place of silence (Matt. 6:6).

St Paul teaches us the same truth. After his profound conversion experience on the road to Damascus where he met the Risen Lord and realised that as a result his whole life was going to be turned upside down, what happened first? He went blind. Darkness overtook him. He had to be led by the hand into the city of Damascus and there for three days in the darkness and the silence, he listened to God. Then Ananias was sent to talk things through with him and Paul was baptised. He knew his life could never be the same again. It would have to be rethought and replanned. So, what did he do? We are told in the letter to the Galatians that he went away, by himself, into Arabia for three years (1:17). Arabia is the desert, the wilderness, the place of silence. There, listening to God, Paul began to envisage his future great missionary career.

Our Lady Mary has the same message for us. She is above everything else a woman of silence. Very few of her words have been recorded but the ones we do have are of infinite significance. So much was happening which she could not fully understand. She was greatly puzzled and at times distressed. So, what did she do? St Luke tells us, and he is so anxious to emphasise it that he tells us twice over, 'As for Mary, she treasured all these things and pondered them in her heart' (Luke 2:19, 52). And when we see her at the foot of the cross, a silent figure, standing rigid, saying nothing, it is imposs-ible for us to penetrate the depths of all that was going on in her heart. It is as if she said to us, 'Be still brother, be still sister. We have no need of words, my son and I'.

And today, God still does great things for us in the silence and the darkness. Think of the presence of the Risen Christ in the Holy Sacrament of the altar. We gaze at the Host and the chalice when they are lifted at Mass; we gaze at the Host when we receive it in Holy Communion; we gaze at it exposed in the monstrance; we kneel before it in the tabernacle. It is Jesus, dwelling in our midst and coming into our hearts in absolute silence. And there is darkness too: darkness of mind because we cannot fully understand or comprehend how this miracle can take place, the miracle of the presence of the Risen Christ in his Body and Blood.

So, we need silence and darkness if we are to hear God speaking to us. We don't normally hear him audibly. It is as we sit in darkness of mind, as we reflect on the mystery of God, who is beyond all understanding, as we listen to the silence that we become aware of what God is wanting us to do. Sometimes we are bewildered, so we have to run to someone for help, perhaps a priest just as Samuel ran to Eli, especially when God seems to be suggesting something which seems very difficult and almost beyond us.

Here is an exercise in silent prayer.

Silent prayer

1. Sit comfortably – back straight – feet flat on the floor – hands on knees – palms down (or turned up).

2. Beginning with the forehead, think slowly about each part of your body in turn from head to foot, and as you think about it let the tension run out. As you do this, reflect on how wonderfully God has created our bodies, saying silently to yourself, over and over, some such words as: Your hands have made and fashioned me, O God; or, I am fearfully and wonderfully made.

3. Listen to the external sounds (traffic, birds, people talking, a distant radio) – concentrate on the sound. Soak it in until it becomes part of you and is no longer a distraction. The sounds are being made by your fellow human beings. Take them all into your heart. We are all bound together in the 'bundle of life'.

4. Listen to the sound of your own breathing. Breathe deeply and slowly, perhaps saying the word 'Father' or 'Jesus' as you breathe in and saying it again as you breathe out. It makes us realise we are totally dependent on God for being kept in life. He is continually filling us with his breath, his Spirit. 'When you let your breath go forth, O God, we are made'; repeat the words

over and over rhythmically in time with your breathing.

5. Think deep down into the centre of your heart, the ground of your being. God is dwelling there in *total silence*. You can't see him, you can't hear him, you can't feel him, you can't understand him. Listen to the silence of God. He seems to be darkness and obscurity.

Keep on repeating quietly to yourself some such phrase as:

Be still and know that I am God.
Wait thou still O my soul upon God.
Commune with your own heart and within your
    chamber and be still.

All this needs is practice. It does not need any special gift. Everyone can do it and it is a matter of perseverance, of going on and on, especially when you feel, 'Oh, it's getting me nowhere. I can't do it'. Go on doing it and you will find, after a time, that it becomes almost automatic and whenever you settle down for your prayer time, you can enter into the silence of God within you. As you persevere, you will find that you can begin to do it sitting on the bus or the underground, waiting in a queue or washing up. We can enter into the silence of the presence of God within us amidst all the bustle and noise around us.

What if the silence is full of distractions and endless thoughts about this and that come tumbling into the mind. Don't get impatient and cross with yourself and feel you are making a mess of it. Never worry about distractions. For myself I don't try to push them away. I let them run down to the end and after that the silence returns.

I think one of the best descriptions of silent prayer and listening to God is given to us by St Teresa of Avila. Her books on prayer and spirituality, although written hundreds of years ago, are still fresh for the twentieth century. She told us to think of our prayer like a river. The surface of the river sometimes runs beautifully, sparkling in the sunshine, rippling smoothly along. Sometimes it is full of rubbish and refuse. Sometimes the surface is stormy, full of spray, flooding over the banks. Sometimes it is absolutely stagnant, covered in scum and looking lifeless. But whatever the state of the surface, underneath the river is flowing smoothly and swiftly down to the sea. This is a perfect picture of our experience in prayer. The surface of the mind is like the surface of the river. It changes. But underneath, always, our heart is wanting to go straight to God, otherwise we would not be trying to pray at all. It is the desire in the heart that matters. Our desire is for God. He sees our desire for him and is not interested in the buzzing flies of distraction. So, think of that river when you are next feeling cross with the distraction and keep going.

2

Familiar Ground
The Lord's Prayer

Our Father, who art in Heaven,
hallowed be thy name;
thy Kingdom come;
thy will be done,
on earth as it is in Heaven.
Give us this day our daily bread.
And forgive us our trespasses,
as we forgive those who trespass against us.
And lead us not into temptation;
but deliver us from evil.
For thine is the Kingdom, the power and the glory,
for ever and ever. Amen.

For many of us the Lord's Prayer has become too familiar. We have said it since we were children and we rattle it off like a parrot. If we pause and reflect on what we are saying, we realise the implications of the words are vast, almost overwhelming, demanding, and sometimes frightening, because they cover every aspect of our relationship with God and with each other.

Our Father

The temptation is to reduce the Lord's Prayer to a personal prayer and to think of it in terms of, '*My* Father . . . forgive *me my* trespasses . . . etc.', when in fact in the word '*our*' we embrace the whole world. God is the beginning and the end of the whole human race. In the word 'our' we gather together all those we love and like, those with whom we live, and worship, and work. We think of those of whom we are frightened, those who threaten us and treat us badly. The word 'our' goes deep down into the world of human distress: the tension of those in marital discord, the cries of the unwanted, the silent screams of the aborted, the sighs of the starving – every aspect of our inhumanity to our fellow human beings. The whole bundle of life is wrapped together in the word 'our'.

We call God 'Father' because Our Lord always did. Yet God is our Mother too. A father protects and a

mother nourishes. God is *All*. He has no gender and
our finite minds cannot begin to grasp this mystery.
To address God as either 'father' or 'mother' is to
think of him in terms of a parent, as indeed in one
sense he is. The Christian religion is the only
one which dares to be so familiar with God. In childhood we are meant to find total security in our
parents; they are a source of happiness and joy, they
are always there, they will find the solution to all
our distresses and questions, they will forgive as
soon as we say 'sorry'. They never let us down. In a
similar way our relationship with God is childlike
and he 'dandles us on his knee'.

Tragically, in Western society today, for many
children the word 'father' or 'mother' has a bad
image. It evokes a memory of someone who deserted
them and so jeopardised their sense of security. The
children of broken homes can have difficulty in
relating to God as 'father' or 'mother'. It depends on
which parent they live with and their relationship
with the parent from whom they have been sepa-
rated. It is difficult for the mind to eradicate long,
deep, emotional wounding.

Who art in Heaven
It is interesting that at the beginning of the prayer
our thoughts are directed to the goal of all Christian
living. Heaven is what we are hoping for as the days,

20

the months and the years flee away behind us. As Thérèse of Lisieux said, 'Eternity is coming towards us in great strides'. We look forward to eternal life when we shall finally become the person God created us to be and our relationship with him and all those who have gone before us will be fulfilled and no longer shadowed by our selfishness and our inhibitions. Heaven is our real *home* and in the familiar hymns we sing there is nearly always a reference to our longing and desire to be there. The saints sigh for it and so St Bernard writes, 'O sweet and blessed country [Heaven] when shall I see your face?'

Christians try to see world events and the happenings of their own lives against the perspective of Heaven. This is the reason why the thinking of Christians about present-day issues (for example, abortion, the sale of armaments, marriage and family life) is different from general attitudes. It is a good habit at the end of a day to review it and try to see all the people we have related to and all the happenings of the day, both small and unexpected, in the context of Heaven. In the Gospels Our Lord places great emphasis on 'watching' and 'being ready' for our final journey through the experience of physical death into the realm of eternity.

Hallowed be thy name

What kind of thoughts come into our minds when we take these words upon our lips? What does 'hallowed' mean? To call God 'Father' means we can be as familiar with him as a child with his or her parents. Yet there is another aspect of God. Our finite minds cannot begin to grasp the infinity of God. God is incomprehensible. We speak of his 'Greatness', his 'Wonder', his 'Glory', his 'Omnipotence', his 'Omniscience', and yet these are only glimpses of the fact the he is *All*. We gaze out into the heavens at night and see the moon, the myriads of stars, the whole world of space stretching on and on and on and yet we believe that God holds it all within the hollow of his hand. The thought is overwhelming. We cannot grasp it. We feel full of awe. We feel no more than a grain of sand upon the seashore. How can we matter to God? Like the psalmist we cry out, 'What is man, O God, that thou art mindful of him?' God is the great *mystery* before whom we fall down in amazement, awe and wonder. All we can do as we reflect on this, is utter those three short, sharp exclamations of adoration which we use every time we attend the Eucharist, 'holy, holy, holy'. They are the three great *O*s of awe and wonder. To do this is to hallow God's name.

22

Thy Kingdom come

Where is God's Kingdom? Ever since the dawn of Christianity Christians have argued and discussed about what the Kingdom of God means. Some say it has nothing to do with this world for Heaven is the Kingdom of God. Others think that we ought to be trying to bring the Kingdom of God into this world. Yet others say only the baptised, those who form the One, Holy, Catholic and Apostolic Church, can speak of themselves as members of the Kingdom of God, whether it be on this side of the grave or the next. Our Lord said, 'the Kingdom of God is within you'. The debate will continue.

Yet whatever our definition there will be one common characteristic: the Kingdom of God will be a place of unity and reconciliation, and in this we know that we have failed. If, as Jesus said, it is 'within us', we are well aware that we all live in a state of inner conflict and warfare. If it is in this world we have only to read the newspaper or watch the news on the television to realise the world is seething with division, violence and strife. If it is the Church, we know that also is splintered into different denominations, which regard each other with suspicion and distrust leading to bigotry and fanaticism. The Church presents to the world the bleeding, broken body of Christ on the cross instead of the wholeness of the risen body of Christ.

Thy will be done on earth as it is in Heaven

It is curious how we always think we know what other people ought to do. We say, 'You should have done that', 'you have made a mistake', 'you have made the wrong decision', 'you have got it all wrong'. We love interfering in other people's lives, trying to take control and even presuming to say, 'This is what God wants you to do!' Is this our way of trying to escape from what God is asking us to do? What is the will of God for your life and mine? What is he asking of us at this moment? We are all at different stages on our pilgrimage to Heaven. God is asking different things of each one of us and we make excuses: 'Oh, we can't do that. It is going to upset our lives. What would people say?' Is he calling you to be a priest, to be a monk or a nun? Is he asking you to put your marriage right, to create a Christian home and to get your relationships right with other people? Is he questioning you about the use of your money and your self-centred existence? What is his will for us? We make so many excuses. We cannot bear the inconvenience of taking God seriously, because it might mean the turning of our lives inside out and taking great risks with our security. Yes, it will mean being like our Blessed Mother Mary who risked everything, the whole of her future happiness and her marriage to Joseph. She did not know what was going to happen to her; she risked being stoned to death for her apparent unfaithfulness to Joseph during the time of their betrothal. She risked everything rather than resist what God was asking of her. Are we prepared to take such risks? If not, why do we keep saying in the Lord's Prayer 'Thy will be done', if we have no intention of facing up to what God is asking of us?

Give us this day our daily bread

When I say these words I become deeply troubled and overwhelmed with a great sense of guilt, because I know that here in the Western world we have far more bread, far more food and far more things than we really need. We have so much in the Western world. We have come to regard luxuries as necessities. The supermarkets are stocked with such a vast and bewildering choice of things to eat that it is almost obscene. We have so much and yet at the same time we know that the majority of people in the world have so little and are living on the breadline or at starvation level. We view the distressing scenes on the television of those living in dire straits of poverty and disease and we feel helpless. What can we do? The problem seems insoluble. God provides enough food for everyone to have sufficient and yet this great imbalance exists. We must all accept the blame for not being able to share what God has given us. We give what we can to all kinds of relief and aid schemes, and it is our Christian duty to do so, and yet we know such schemes only provide a necessary cosmetic and do not plumb the depths of the problem.

How has this intolerable situation arisen? It is due to bad, selfish systems of economy. These systems are devised by those in political power, those we elect to represent us in Parliament. It is our bounden duty to question our prospective Members of Parliament about their plans to redress this terrible situation in which we in the West claim the far greater share of God's abundance at the expense of the destitute and the starving. The Lord's Prayer is not an escape route from the problems of this world but an impetus to seek their solution.

In the West we are such waste-makers. Our lack of care in the things we throw away, particularly food, is a slap in the face to God the Giver. I am always fascinated by one small detail in the familiar story of Our Lord feeding the five thousand. At the end, when everyone had had sufficient, Our Lord did not say, as we would probably have done, 'we can leave the crumbs and leftovers for the birds and animals'. Our Lord said no such thing. He commanded, 'Pick up the pieces left over, so that nothing gets wasted' (John 6:12). There must be no waste but every scrap of what God gives must be used for the right ends.

When we say, 'Give us this day our daily bread', are we only referring to the food we eat at breakfast, lunch, tea, dinner? Does it not also refer to that other bread, to that food and drink which is vital to maintaining our life with God – the bread of life, the cup of salvation, the Blessed Sacrament, the Body and Blood of Christ. We have to ask ourselves if we are full of longing and desire to receive the life of Christ in the Holy Sacrament every single day? Can we say with the psalmist, 'O God, you are my God, I am seeking you, my soul is thirsting for you?' (Ps. 63:1) I always remember once, when I was staying in Malta, meeting the Chief of Police in the island just before he was to retire. I asked him, 'Have you any plans for your retirement?' 'Well', he said, 'my job has made it so difficult to get to Mass every day. All my life I have prayed "Give us this day our daily bread", and now at last I look forward to being able to put it into practice with daily Holy Communion.' I couldn't help wondering how many other people facing their retirement would have said that? That Chief of Police had got the right perspective on life. He was seeing his life against the background of eternity. This is what really matters.

*Forgive us our trespasses, as we forgive those
who trespass against us*

What should we Christians be most noted for, in the
family where we live, in the place where we work,
in the clubs where we take our recreation, in the
congregation where we worship? What makes us
different? Surely, we are those who know how to
forgive. We Christians are the forgiving people. We
don't forgive once or twice but over and over again.
Our Lord made this very clear to St Peter (Matt.
18:22). Peter felt a bit indignant that he should have
to go on forgiving, and so he said to Jesus, 'How
often should I forgive?' Our Lord replied, 'Seventy
times seven', which means always, always, always.
It has to be forgiveness without strings. There are
some people who will say, 'Well, I will forgive if you
do this, that or the other'. There are no conditions
attached to Christian forgiveness. We have the marvellous example of Zacchaeus, the little man who
climbed up into a tree because he was too small to
see Our Lord otherwise (Luke 19:1–10). He looked
down at Our Lord and Our Lord looked up at him.
Zacchaeus loved money. He was a tax collector and
had no scruples about forcing people to pay up while
adding on an extra bonus for himself, even if it
meant reducing people to poverty. He had no mercy.
When Our Lord looked up at him he didn't say, 'Now,
Zacchaeus, if you will stop behaving in this way

I will forgive you.' He accepted Zacchaeus just as he was, and said, 'Zacchaeus, come down. I want to come home and have lunch with you today.' Zacchaeus was accepted just as he was, in spite of his ill-gotten gains. It was only after he had been accepted and after they had lunched together that Zacchaeus began to put things right and try to make amends for his avarice. We all have to learn, when we are forgiving others, first of all to accept them as they are, with all their weaknesses, addictions and 'hang-ups', their peculiarities and their tempers, their depressions and their idiosyncrasies. After all, we expect other people to accept us as we are. Only after we are accepted (loved) can we begin to change. Some people cannot even forgive themselves. They have a very poor self-image. Yet it is impossible to forgive others until we have first accepted ourselves as we are, with all our flaws and failures. Neither do we have to earn our forgiveness from God. He accepts us as we are because he loves us. After all, when the Prodigal Son returned home, his father did not wait to find out whether he was sorry or not before he ran to embrace him and accept him, in spite of all that had happened (Luke 15:11–24). St Luke writes of it so beautifully: 'While he [the prodigal son] was still a long way off, his father saw him and was moved with pity. He ran to the boy, clasped him in his arms and kissed him tenderly' (v. 20). Only then, after being accepted as he was, did the son make his confession.

And lead us not into temptation

To put it simply, help us to say 'no' when the Evil One is being persuasive. Nevertheless, we so often, quite deliberately, walk headlong into situations of temptation. We go to places, knowing before we go that they will have a bad influence on us. When we get there we may drink too much and eat too much, and spend more money than we can afford. We indulge in gossip and back down in conversation from bearing witness to the truths of our Christian faith.

We let envy drive us into false destructive criticism and our laughter is unkind. We try to dominate and manipulate others and are often contemptuous ... the tale is never-ending and we are all tainted by it.

But deliver us from evil

Are we living in very evil times? I don't think the times of today are more evil than any in the past. The problem only seems greater because there are more people living in the world today. The media seems to delight in bringing to our notice every aspect of evil. It comes tumbling into our sitting-rooms on the television screen. St Augustine of Hippo said, 'If the times are evil it is because we have made them so'. Yes, the times are evil, but they have always been evil. The trouble is that it rubs off on us. We condemn the evil and yet we are fascinated by it, contaminated, mesmerised and infected by it. So we begin to waver and wobble in our Christian point of view. We make excuses and don't like to stand up and be counted, mocked and derided because our views are not those of the multitude.

The storms of evil blowing around us are very fierce:

the culture of death in the quest for abortion, the desire for euthanasia and the 'careers rather than babies' climate;

the obsession with every kind of sexual experience: sex devoid of responsibility;

the worship of money and possessions: the avalanche of guessing and 'knowledge' games on the television, not played for the pleasure of the game but for the glittering prizes;

the need for everything to be 'instant', not only in food and the relief of pain, but also instant happiness in marriage;

the long trail of broken marriages, broken homes; unwanted and abused children;

the excessive individualism whereby everyone decides for themselves what is right and what is wrong, irrespective of the suffering it causes others;

the scorn of virginity, both male and female;
the hypnotic effect of the world of advertising
whereby we are manipulated into buying things we
don't need often for the sake of status;
the destruction of the environment motivated by
greed;
the manufacture and the sale of deadly armaments
which we know will be used for tyrannical ends;
the 'meaninglessness' which haunts so many, once
the glitter of secularism has grown tarnished and
pointless;
the extremes of wealth and poverty;
the upsurge of violent behaviour and the tensions
of racism.

All this and more. We cannot help but be influenced by it. So we need to say with great fervour,
'Lord, deliver us from evil'. Christians must have
the ability to identify completely with the world in
its need and the power to overcome the world at its
strongest.

Such are the words Our Lord gave us when he
taught us how to pray. Their implications are far-
reaching, covering every man, woman and child and
our relationships with each other and God as we
journey on to the goal of fulfilment in Heaven. 'O
grant us life that shall not end in our true native
land with you' (St Thomas Aquinas).

In the very early days of the Church, the first Christians added another sentence to the Lord's Prayer. Sometimes we use it and sometimes not. It is always said at the Catholic Mass: 'For thine is the Kingdom, the power and the glory, for ever and ever. Amen.' These words set the whole of the prayer firmly into its right context. It is the context of eternity, the background of the glory and wonder of God, who has no beginning and no end, who always has been and always will be, who is an eternal *now*.

The Lord's Prayer covers all prayer. It will suffice if, each day, having got ourselves still, and having thought of all those for whom we ought and want to pray, and gathering them all up in the word 'Our', we say the rest of the prayer very slowly and reflectively. We can pray it anywhere: commuting, sitting in the bus, underground or train, driving the car, walking in the street, sitting at home or in church. However, wherever we say it, there is no place for glibly, unthinkingly and speedily rattling off the words Our Lord gave us to prepare us for Heaven.

3

An Angel Spoke
The Hail Mary Prayer

Hail Mary, full of grace!
The Lord is with you.
Blessed are you among women,
and blessed is the fruit of your womb, Jesus.
Holy Mary, Mother of God, pray for us sinners,
now and at the hour of our death. Amen.

The first half of the Hail Mary prayer, which is taken from St Luke's Gospel (1:29 and 42), is older than the Lord's Prayer. The first sentence was spoken by God himself through his messenger, the Archangel Gabriel.

Hail Mary, full of grace!

Mary was full of graciousness, full of gratitude. Her song of gratitude, the Magnificat (Luke 1:46–55), shows how easily and spontaneously gratitude to God springs to her lips. It rises above the bewilderment and the problems stemming from what God was asking her to do (Luke 1:34). It is a rebuke to our ingratitude to God. So often we approach God with groans, sighs, fears and complaints. We take all the infinite daily blessings we receive from God for granted. Sometimes we even grumble about them, for example the food we eat! As we rise each morning from the 'death' of sleep into a new day, do we get up 'singing for joy', and do we turn out the light at night full of gratitude for all God's blessings during the day?

Mary had an extra grace, given her by God, which we do not have. When Mary was conceived, through the love of her parents Joachim and Anne, God stepped in and prepared her to be the mother of his Son. We, at our conception, inherit the sins and failings of our parents and all our forefathers before

37

us, and we call this original sin (the stain inherited from belonging to the human race). In the Immaculate Conception, as it is known, God kept Mary free from original sin. We are only freed from the stain of inherited sin when the waters of baptism wash it away. Mary, by the unique intervention of God, was pre-baptised at her conception, years before Our Lord instituted the sacrament of baptism for the rest of us. She was indeed born full of grace. But she was still a human being, like us in that she was free to make her own choice. God may have specially prepared her to be fit to be the mother of his Son, but he could not force her to accept this role. She was free to refuse. When the request came from the Archangel Gabriel, the problems and difficulties Mary had to face were enormous, but grace prevailed and she said 'yes' (Luke 1:38).

The Lord is with you

The Lord is also with us. God claimed us at our baptism. His Spirit came to dwell within us. We are the temples of the Holy Spirit. God is just as close to us as he was to Mary. Mary responded to the fact that she (like us) was fashioned in the image of God. She was attentive to the Spirit within her, totally open and responsive, like wax in the hands of God. We are not. God dwells within us, just as closely as he dwelt in Mary, but unlike her we do not respond to what God is asking of us. We make excuses or we make 'conditions', or we try to persuade God to say 'yes' to what we want to do. The Lord within us asks penetrating questions about what we are doing with the life he gave us? How are we going to build up our married and family life? Are we falling a prey to materialistic and secular influences? Are we letting the spirit of the age swamp the Spirit of God within us? Have we forgotten 'the Lord is with us'? Mary let God take over in her pilgrimage to Heaven. We prefer to be in control ourselves and to make up our own minds as to what is right. Like Adam and Eve we want to be as God. The result is total disintegration. The 'Lord is with you' has been trampled upon and it would be more truthful to say, 'You are on your own now!'

Blessed are you among women, and blessed is the fruit of your womb, Jesus

These are the words uttered by Elizabeth, the cousin of Mary and the mother-to-be of John the Baptist. Mary had gone to visit her, to share her great secret that she was to be the mother of Jesus. She felt Elizabeth would understand (Luke 1:39–45). Elizabeth gave 'a loud cry' when she welcomed Mary and said, 'Blessed are you among women and blessed is the fruit of your womb'. The word 'blessed' means 'special': Mary had surrendered herself totally to

39

God to do what he wanted and so she is a source of inspiration to us all. Mary is the most 'special' of all Christians. As she spoke, Elizabeth was looking back over all the famous women of the Old Testament whom God had used and who had co-operated with him in the fulfilment of his plans – the Sarahs, the Rachels, the Miriams, the Ruths, the Rebeccas, the Rahabs, the Hannahs, the Deborahs, the Esthers, the Judiths – all leading up to Mary, who is the crown. When we say the prayer we have in mind not only the remarkable women of the Old Testament, but also all the wonderful Christian women since Mary – the Magdalenes, the Agathas, the Teresas, the Clares, the Hildas, the Agneses and the Margarets. Yet Mary still remains the crown. She is the most remarkable and unique woman in the whole history of the world.

The name *Jesus* is both the climax and the centre-point of the whole prayer. Only because of Jesus, only because of the far-flung implications of his birth, death, resurrection and ascension, does the prayer have any meaning at all. Jesus was just as much the Saviour of Mary as he is of us. How lovely that the name of Jesus should be at the centre of the prayer, that saving name, which has meant so much to countless Christians through the centuries and means so much to us and above all means so much to Mary. 'How sweet the name of Jesus sounds in a believer's ear' (from a hymn by John Newton, 1725–1807).

So far the prayer has been words from the Bible, but now it changes and there is added a human cry, a cry from the heart. It is a cry which all sons and daughters make to their human mothers, in full expectation that it will be answered. Mary was given to us all at the cross to be our heavenly Mother (John 19:25–7) and so we say:

Holy Mary, Mother of God, pray for us sinners, now and at the hour of our death

Why not just 'Holy Mary, pray for us'? Why add the definition 'Mother of God'? A great theological statement is being affirmed, which safeguards that essential truth of the Christian faith enshrined in the Creed. Mary's child is not just a specially good man, living for others, a pale imitation of God, but is God himself,

> We believe in one Lord, Jesus Christ, the only Son of God, eternally begotten of the Father, God from God, Light from Light, true God from true God, begotten, not made, of one being with the Father. (The Nicene Creed)

It also tells us something about God. He waited for and was dependent on the co-operation of a human being, a human mother, before he could come into our midst. He never forces himself upon us but waits for our free response to his suggestions. So what a debt we owe to Mary for her 'yes' to God.

'Pray for us sinners'. These words bring us down to earth with a bump! Our human condition is one of unworthiness. St Paul echoes our own experience when he writes, '. . . But I am unspiritual; I have been sold as a slave to sin. I cannot understand my own behaviour. I fail to carry out the things I want to do, and I find myself doing the very things I hate' (Rom. 7:14–16). 'Kyrie eleison' should be our attitude before God: 'forgive us our trespasses as we forgive those who trespass against us'; 'Jesus Christ, Son of the Living God, have mercy upon us'. Mercifully God accepts us as we are. We do not have to earn his love. We know that like Jesus, our Mother Mary will listen. Mothers always do. They don't hold the failings of their children against them.

'Pray for us . . . now and at the hour of our death'. These are the only two things we are sure of: the present moment and the fact that one day we shall die. Everything inbetween is totally unknown. Yes, we make plans, but we can never be sure that they will materialise. It is reassuring to think of Mary, at the moment of our dying, supporting us with her prayer, welcoming us and taking us, as she always does, to Jesus.

It is important to remember that the Hail Mary prayer, like the Lord's Prayer, is all in the plural. It speaks of 'us' and 'our', not 'me' and 'my'. When we say it, we gather the whole of humanity and place it in Mary's arms. She is the universal Mother. We pray with her and she with us, and we look forward to the day when, with her, we shall adore the mystery, the wonder and the glory of the Trinity of God. The Trinity, who as yet is in 'light inaccessible, hid from our eyes' (from the hymn 'Immortal, invisible, God only wise' by W. C. Smith, 1824–1908).

4

The Pen of the Spirit
Praying with the Bible

When the Spirit of truth comes,
he will lead you to the complete truth.
                              (John 16:13)

In this chapter I am going to consider three ways of praying with the Bible. For each of these it is important, after choosing a passage, to get still and ask the Holy Spirit to direct your reading and pondering. Then read the passage slowly and reflectively. A good example of a passage to start with is the story of blind Bartimaeus:

The blind man of Jericho

They reached Jericho; and as he left Jericho with his disciples and a large crowd, Bartimaeus (that is, the son of Timaeus), a blind beggar, was sitting at the side of the road. When he heard that it was Jesus of Nazareth, he began to shout and to say, 'Son of David, Jesus, have pity on me.' And many of them scolded him and told him to keep quiet, but he only shouted all the louder, 'Son of David, have pity on me.' Jesus stopped and said, 'Call him here.' So they called the blind man. 'Courage,' they said 'get up; he is calling you.' So throwing off his cloak, he jumped up and went to Jesus. Then Jesus spoke, 'What do you want me to do for you?' 'Rabbi,' the blind man said to him 'Master, let me see again.' Jesus said to him, 'Go, your faith has saved you.' And immediately his sight returned and he followed him along the road. (Mark 10:46–52)

(1) Praying with the mind

Bartimaeus was blind. We may not have to suffer physical blindness but there are many other ways in which we can be blind. We can be very blind about ourselves and about others.

We can be blind to the obvious, particularly about the truths of the Christian faith. So, we say about someone, 'He can't see for looking'. This was so often true of the twelve apostles. There was Jesus in front of them; they lived with him, travelled with him, ate with him and yet he had so often to say to them about his teaching, 'Don't you understand?' 'Have you no perception?' 'Are your minds closed?' 'Don't you remember the feeding of the five thousand, for example!' 'Have you eyes that do not see, ears that do not hear?'

Do we really want to let the light of Christ into our lives? Will it be more than we can take? Sometimes people tell us something about ourselves and we don't like it; we are surprised and we may at the time object, push it away and justify ourselves. If we are sensible we shall say nothing; we will look at what they have said, and ponder and reflect on it. After all, the very vigour of our denial is not without significance! We may have to recognise that it is true and say, 'My eyes have been opened. Before I was blind. Now I see.' We should be grateful too, because every growth in self-knowledge is one step nearer to God. Yet how we dislike being made to see. How many relationships break down because those involved cannot bear to hear the truth about themselves from each other? Friendships too founder on this rock. Not only are we blind about ourselves, but also very blind to the needs of others, sometimes deliberately so, because to allow ourselves to see could be very inconvenient and could demand sacrifice.

Sometimes we connive at making others blind. 'Pulling the wool over his/her eyes' is the term we use and we do it because we want to avoid situations we would rather not look at or do anything about.

How many of us too, even among those who outwardly are totally committed to Christianity, are blind to the priority and need of prayer in the Christian life? Yet without regular and sustained prayer our whole relationship with God breaks down, and Christian structures and practices cease to give out the light they should.

Bartimaeus began to shout. His importunity is emphasised by the fact that he shouted. He was determined to be heard. It recalls very vividly Our Lord's instruction, 'Ask and you will receive, knock and it will be opened to you' (Luke 11:9–13). Are we importunate with God? Perhaps we are, and yet so often our asking is self-centred. We decide first what will be best for ourselves and for others and then ask God for that. We are really praying, 'let my will be done', when the very essence of Christian prayer both for ourselves and others is, 'thy will be done'. God's will may often seem to run quite contradictory to what we understand or desire and of course we can resist it because we are free. God sees us always within the perspective of eternity and his will for us is shaped against this background . . . if we will allow it. So often what he gives or allows now, both for ourselves and others, we cannot fully understand. One day when we enter our heavenly glorified life everything will become abundantly clear. Our life on earth is like the wrong side of a piece of tapestry, all knots and seeming muddle and confusion, but on the right side (our life in heaven) a beautiful and perfect design is being worked out.

' . . . And many of them scolded him and told him to keep quiet'. Curious, isn't it? Why didn't they want him to be helped, and why didn't they lead him to Jesus? I fear they were all too human, they were 'up front', enjoying Jesus and listening to him; they did not want Bartimaeus' interruption, however justified it was, to make them lose his attention. We know all about that, don't we? Possessiveness of people, jobs and situations: who of us has not been burdened by it?

In the end they gave way and said to Bartimaeus, 'he is calling you'. We know Jesus is always doing this. He is calling us every day to commit ourselves to the promises of our baptism, calling us perhaps to the priesthood or monastic life, calling us to teaching or nursing, calling us to Christian marriage or the uprooting of something in our lives which is spoiling our relationship with him. There is always something but we need courage to face up to it. Curiously that is what the crowd said to Bartimaeus, 'Courage, get up; he is calling you'. Why did it need such courage to go and be cured of his blindness? Why the hesitation? Nevertheless we are told he jumped up and threw off his cloak – a strange little touch which adds to the authenticity of the story. Why should he throw off his cloak? Is this gesture a symbol of the things we all have to throw off and leave behind when we respond to the call of Jesus? . . . Sometimes warm, comforting and familiar things, like a cloak, that we are loathe to surrender.

Even more curious are Jesus' first words to Bartimaeus, 'What do you want me to do for you?' Wasn't it obvious? Bartimaeus wanted his sight back. 'Let me see again' (so he had not been born blind). 'What do you want me to do for you?' This is a direct question being put to each one of us too. What do I want Jesus to do for me? It is a searching question to which it is all too easy to give a superficial answer. We are afraid to ask for something which might have costing implications. Jesus puts the weight of the choice on us. He respects our freedom. He does not say, 'I think this will be best for you'. He does know what will be best for us, but he is not going to force it. Love never compels.

' . . . Your faith has saved you'. It is curious that Jesus did not say, 'your faith has healed you' or 'your faith has restored your sight'. Instead he used the word 'saved'. Saved him from what? It makes us ask, 'Is there anything I need saving from?' How would I explain in simple terms to someone who asked me, 'What do you Christians mean by the word "salvation"?'

Jesus said to Bartimaeus, 'Go', but Bartimaeus didn't go. Instead he 'followed Jesus along the road'. This was an immediate decision, freely made. Jesus gave him the opportunity not to follow but to go away without any sense of guilt. This makes us look again at our own 'following' and how far it is tangled up with a web of compromises of our own wilful weaving.

So far we have been using our minds to reflect on the Bartimaeus story to discover what God is saying to us today about our relationship with him. You may retort, 'That's fine for those who have a quick and alert mind, but my eyes slip over the words and not a thing jumps out of them for me!' Don't despair, there are other ways of praying with the story.

(2) *Praying with the senses*

Read the story. Close your eyes: picture the scene. What do you *see*?

Such a multitude of things: the crowd, the different colours of the clothes people are wearing, the children, the road, the countryside, the hills in the distance, the vegetation, the clouds, the blazing sun, Jesus himself and Bartimaeus.

What do you *hear*?

Bartimaeus crying out, shouting louder and louder, the crowd telling him to be quiet and then changing their minds; the shuffling of people's feet, the leaves of the trees fluttering in the breeze, the children playing among themselves, the voice of Jesus.

What do you *feel*?

The heat of the sun, the breeze on your face, some of the crowd pushing against you.

What do you *smell*?

People's bodies sweating in the heat, some of the women are wearing perfume.

What do you *taste*?

The dust rising from the shuffling of so many

people's feet has got into your mouth and nostrils, it tastes gritty.

Now put yourself into the picture. Where do you want to be? Close up to Jesus? Near to Bartimaeus? Hidden in the middle of the crowd so Jesus won't notice you? Standing some distance away, not wanting to be involved? Why have you chosen your particular position? Does it tell you anything about your relationship with Jesus?

(3) Repetitive praying

If your mind is not very active or your imagination not very fertile, the above two methods of praying will not be very helpful. It doesn't matter and don't try to force them. You may be a more contemplative 'gazing' type of person. Read the passage through. Are there any particular phrases or words which strike you? Obvious ones would be Jesus' question to Bartimaeus, 'What do you want me to do for you?', or the crowd saying to Bartimaeus, 'Courage, get up; he is calling you', or the words of Bartimaeus, 'Master, let me see again'. Whatever phrase you choose, say it slowly and reflectively over and over again for five, ten or fifteen minutes, counting on your fingers or the beads of a rosary. It may produce new thoughts about your relationship with Jesus, or jolt you into some decision, or it may simply be a blank gazing on Jesus or Bartimaeus which cannot be described.

Always keep in mind the words of St Teresa of Avila that, 'Hurry is the death of all prayer'.

5

Hide and Seek

Praying with Mary and the Saints

I will seek him whom my heart loves.
(Song of Songs 3:2)

Most of us, in our homes, have collections of family photographs. We have albums of special family occasions, such as weddings, baptisms and holidays. One of the wonderful things about going into a church, particularly if it is a Catholic church, is to find oneself surrounded by the family pictures of all the baptised. By baptism we all became brothers and sisters in that worldwide family of the One, Holy, Catholic and Apostolic Church. We make pictures of our best loved brothers and sisters. We depict them in stained glass, sculpt them in stone and plaster, paint them on ikons and carve them in wood. They are the Church's family photographs: of Francis, Benedict, Peter and Paul, Anthony and Joseph; of Teresa, Bernadette, Agnes, Hilda and, above all, of Mary the mother of Jesus, among the many other saints. We are all intimately related to each other through our baptism when we became grafted into Christ. We are all one great family, on earth, in Purgatory and in Heaven. Death does not cut us off from those who have gone before us. At death, life is changed, not taken away. Our relationship with God becomes deeper, we come closer to our own dear departed ones and we relate to the saints more intimately. We shall see 'the things that no eye has seen and no ear has heard, things beyond the mind of man, all that God has prepared for those who love him' (1 Cor. 2:9).

At the Eucharist we are one great family together, on earth and in Heaven, gathered round the altar, adoring Jesus. We ask the saints to help us and support us with their prayers. We don't pray *to* the saints. They are not gods and goddesses, but human beings like ourselves. If I say to you, 'Next Thursday I've got a very important interview and I feel nervous about it, will you please support me with your prayers', I am not praying *to* you but asking you to pray *with* me and *for* me. This is the kind of relationship we have with the saints and with Mary, the mother of Jesus.

We all have our favourite saints. There is a saint to suit every temperament. We should read the lives of the saints and encourage our children to do the same. The cult of the saints is far more important than that of pop stars or tennis champions or soccer players, because the saints bring their influence to bear on us. It is an experience which stretches right through death into eternity.

The top favourite among the saints is Mary, the mother of Jesus. She is a saint plus! We love her because Jesus loves her, and wants us to love her too. She is vital to Christianity, which is why her name is mentioned in the middle of the Creed. It is fascinating to reflect on the mystery of the fact that the whole scheme of Christian redemption depends upon the 'yes' of Mary, the 'yes' of a woman. This is why, in the life of the Church, women have a very special role. It is not the same role as men. It is more 'exalted' because God depended on one woman's willing co-operation before he could come among us to save us.

So, we are surrounded on all sides by the prayers of Mary and the saints. They are giving a triumphant 'yes' to our feeble efforts to live the Christian faith. Since we are, as St Paul reminds us, surrounded 'with so many witnesses in a great cloud on every side of us, we too, then, should throw off everything that hinders us, especially the sin that clings so easily, and keep running steadily in the race we have started' (Heb. 1:1–2). We can never get away from the saints. We may try to ignore them and pretend they are not there, but they are always with us, praying for us and encouraging us.

Our pilgrimage to God in prayer is very much like a game of hide and seek. We keep finding God – sometimes he feels very close, very near – and then at other times he seems to disappear altogether and we have to go searching, seeking and waiting for his return. In fact he never goes away. His presence is not dependent on our 'feelings'. Every finding of him is a new finding and every losing is a new losing. No experience of 'finding' and 'losing' can ever be repeated, because we are all on a journey and changing all the time, growing and developing as we 'put on Christ'.

This experience of hide and seek is wonderfully illustrated in the life of Mary. She found God in a new and special way when she said 'yes' to his request to be the mother of Jesus. Her consent made her the first of all Christians, the first disciple to be near and close to Jesus. The decision was not easy. Although she had been specially prepared by God in her Immaculate Conception – free from that stain of sin we all inherit from our forefathers – yet being a human being and not a goddess, she was free to refuse. We don't find it difficult to refuse some of the things God asks us to do. We can always find excuses which sound rational and full of common sense. We are told by St Luke that Mary was 'deeply disturbed' by God's request (Luke 1:29). What of her future? She was making all her preparations to marry Joseph. How would he react? He knew the child was not his. Would he invoke the extremity of the Jewish law and have her stoned to death for her apparent unfaithfulness to him during their time of betrothal? What would her parents say about it? Would they believe her? She knew what the neigh- bours would say, the kind of snide remarks they would make. 'Look at those two, Mary and Joseph, always so religious, always pretending to be so good. Now look what's happened. There's a baby on the way and they are not even married.' The risks were enormous and Mary risked everything. 'I am the handmaid of the Lord,' said Mary, 'let what you have said be done to me' (Luke 1:38). She cast her bread upon the waters and went out into the unknown. Our redemption depends on her decision. No wonder we love her. No wonder God loves her. No wonder he wants us to love her too.

When we have a big decision to make, we may worry about what to do and discuss it with others (Mary didn't), but when it is finally made there is a great sense of relief. It was like that with Mary. She had made her decision and she felt she wanted to share her secret with someone who might understand. So she set off to visit her cousin Elizabeth, who was pregnant with John the Baptist. St Luke describes the visit so vividly:

> Mary set out at that time and went as quickly as she could to a town in the hill country of Judah. She went into Zechariah's house and greeted Elizabeth. Now as soon as Elizabeth heard Mary's greeting, the child leapt in her womb and Elizabeth was filled with the Holy Spirit.

The Spirit revealed to her what had happened to Mary and so,

She gave a loud cry and said, 'Of all women you are the most blessed, and blessed is the fruit of your womb. Why should I be honoured with a visit from the mother of my Lord? For the moment your greeting reached my ears, the child in my womb leapt for joy. Yes, blessed is she who believed that the promise made by the Lord would be fulfilled.' (1:39–45)

If Mary had had any doubts about her decision, they were now completely swept away. It was a moment of great affirmation. Mary felt so close to God, at that moment, that she was inspired to sing the Magnificat, 'My soul glorifies the Lord . . .' (Luke 1:46–55). This great song of Mary has been repeated down the centuries at the Evening Office. How prophetic it is that, in the middle, Mary had a vision of the centuries to come and sang, 'Henceforth all ages will call me blessed'. It was a moment of great closeness to God, the kind of religious experience which only happens to us, perhaps once or twice in a lifetime.

Such experiences don't last. They didn't with Mary. She was soon brought down to earth with a bump. She had not expected the difficult journey to Bethlehem in the last days of her pregnancy. She certainly had not expected to bring the child to birth in the squalid conditions of a stable. She may have felt rejected that the keeper of the inn could not be bothered to tell the other occupants of her condition and so squeeze her in somewhere. Had she not been told when she promised to bear the child that, 'He will be great and will be called Son of the Most High. The Lord God will give him the throne of his ancestor David; he will rule over the House of David for ever and his reign will have no end ... And so the child will be holy and will be called Son of God' (Luke 1:32,33,36). If this was true, why did she have to bring him into this world among the animals? She may have been bewildered and puzzled, as we all are at times, in our journey to God.

She must have been even more puzzled by the first visitors to the child. The shepherds. Devout Jews (and Mary and Joseph were very devout) tended to look down on shepherds because, owing to the nature of their work, they could not observe all the minute rules and regulations of the Jewish faith. They were definitely at the bottom end of Jewish society. So why were they coming? Why not the religious and devout?

Even more bewildering must have been the visit of the Wise Men (Matt. 2:1–12). They were Gentiles, non-Jews. The Jews thought of themselves as the 'chosen race', specially chosen by God, and therefore non-Jews were akin to second-class citizens. Mary reflected on these things. She did not rush around talking about or discussing them. She was a woman of silence. St Luke is very concerned to emphasise Mary's silence. He refers to it twice: 'Mary . . . treasured all these things and pondered them in her heart' (Luke 2:19) and 'His mother stored up all these things in her heart' (Luke 2:51).

There was worse to follow (Matt. 2:13–23). After the visit of the Wise Men Herod was determined to find the young child and slay him, fearing he might grow up to become a political threat. Mary and Joseph became refugees, fleeing in the middle of the night to Egypt. There was no time for preparation. Neighbours, friends and relations, all that was near and dear to them, had to be left behind at a moment's notice. I don't think any of us can imagine how difficult Mary and Joseph would have found life in Egypt. It was totally abhorrent to Jews to have to live in a situation and atmosphere where pagan idols were worshipped. It was a direct affront to the second commandment given by Moses, 'You shall not make yourself a carved image or any likeness of anything in heaven or on earth beneath or in the waters under the earth; you shall not bow down to them or serve them' (Exod. 20:4). As Mary and Joseph clung to the practice of their Jewish faith, I am sure they often wanted to change the words of Psalm 137 to 'beside the waters of the Nile we sat and wept at the memory of Zion' (Jerusalem) as they looked longingly towards home, to all that Jeru-salem meant to Jews. It was not an easy time for them, perhaps wondering every day, 'Is it safe for us to return yet?' How often people seem to think that Christianity should be a kind of insurance policy against suffering, disaster and pain. It was not like that for Mary, nor is it for any Christian.

At last Mary and Joseph got back home; the child was now a young boy. Some years later, when he was twelve years old, an incident occurred while the family was on pilgrimage to Jerusalem for the Pass-over and Jesus got lost (Luke 2:41–52). For three days Mary and Joseph searched frantically for him. Imagine their state of mind. Had he been hurt? or kidnapped? or murdered? At last they discovered him in the Temple, 'sitting among the doctors, list-ening to them, and asking them questions; and all those who heard him were astounded at his intelli-gence and his replies. They were overcome . . .'. Mary's human-ness and exasperated relief are evident from her words, 'My child, why have you done this to us? See how worried your father and I have been, looking for you.' There are times too when we get exasperated with God and say, 'I cannot think why you are dealing with me in this kind of way? I'm doing the best I can'. It is the sort of remark you find on the lips of St Teresa of Avila. She had to do a great deal of travelling, founding new convents all over Spain. The roads, in her day, were often no more than tracks, mud-ridden and stony. On one occasion, when the coach had overturned once again and she and her sisters found themselves in a muddy ditch, she looked up to Heaven and said, 'Really, God! If this is the way you treat your friends, I'm not surprised you've got so few!' I think we all, at times, feel a kind of exasperation with the situations which can arise because of our commitment to Christ.

After having been found in the Temple, Jesus returned to Nazareth with Mary and Joseph, 'and lived under their authority' (Luke 2:51). For thirty years he lived in obscurity. It was thirty years of humdrum, monotonous village life: the daily work in the carpenter's shop with Joseph, the going to the synagogue on the Sabbath, the talk and the gossip in the market-place in the evening. There was nothing exciting, nothing spectacular about it and not a single word about it has come down to us. Yet it was under these conditions of ordinariness that the relationship between Mary and her son deepened and she began to glimpse and understand who he really was. Perhaps the Son of God spent the greatest part of his earthly life doing very ordinary things because that is the way in which most of us have to spend our lives. Just as it was under those conditions that the relationship between Mary and

Jesus deepened, so with us humdrum daily routine provides an ideal way for growing into God. The sacrifice of Calvary was the fruit of years of self-disciplined faith and obedience in the least exciting or heroic sphere, village life. Minding the sheep, mending the table, fetching the water, hunting for the lost coin: that was the stuff of which the full, perfect and sufficient sacrifice was made. So it will have to be for all of us who, like Mary, want to share the sacrifice and the victory.

Then Jesus left her, left her for his three short years of public life. Did she want him to go? Does a mother ever want her son to go? Mary was human; she was tempted to be possessive and to keep him for herself. Those past, long years had been so wonderful, and she wanted to hang on to them, just as we often want to hang on to the past relationship we had with Jesus, when it all seemed so marvellous. Then it changes. We all get possessive about relationships, about people and about the jobs we do. We won't let go. Mary had to let him go. We are told by St Mark that after his departure she went to look for him (Mark 3:32) and when she found him she had to adjust to a new situation. In Nazareth she had had him all to herself but now she was only another woman on the edge of the crowd. Other people needed him now and wanted to make claims upon him. All she could do now was to accompany him with her prayer.

But at last she found him again. It was the kind of finding she had never anticipated, never wanted. There he hung, between heaven and earth, bleeding, dying. Her maternal anguish was acute. Were these the hands which once clung around her neck in childhood, now smashed by the nails? Were these the feet she first taught to walk, now broken and bleeding? There was nothing she could do except stand silent and helpless, when she really longed to be able to take him down from the cross. Moreover, mingled with her maternal suffering was great spiritual stress. And this was worse. Perhaps she was assailed by every kind of temptation. She had never expected her son's life would end this way and so waves of resentment, bitterness and anger against God may have swept over her and sought to possess her. Why should her son have to suffer in this way? Why should there be such injustice and tyranny? Had she been right in saying 'yes' to God all those years ago when she had assented to bearing his son? Now, as far as she could see, this was the end of everything. She did not know that he was going to rise from the dead. Her whole life, her whole world was collapsing around her feet. Now she knew what Simeon had meant when on the day she had presented her newborn son in the

Temple, he had turned to her and said, 'and a sword will pierce your own soul too' (Luke 2:35).

And yet it was at this moment, this darkest hour, when all seemed lost, that God did a most wonderful thing with Mary. As Jesus hung on the cross, and as he looked down on his mother and, by her side, St John, the only one of his disciples who had not deserted him, he handed Mary over to John's care (John 19:25–7). On the surface this may seem a very normal, compassionate thing to do, but in fact to Jesus' fellow Jews standing round the cross it was a scandal and provocation. One of the most striking aspects of the Jewish faith was its great emphasis on the family. The family cared for its own. Whatever kind of trouble or stress any member of the family was suffering, they would always care for them and never reject them. Yet here was Jesus taking his own mother away from the care of her relations. They would have looked after her. It was a totally un-Jewish idea that she should be taken from them and handed over to the care of someone who was not a blood relation. So John took her to his own home. What did it mean?

She called him 'son' and he called her 'mother'. John was the first of countless millions of Christians down the ages, right down to our own day, who have turned to Mary and said 'mother'. At the cross Mary, by Our Lord's own command, became our mother. It was a ray of light piercing the dark desolation of the cross. Yet, at the time, perhaps neither Mary nor John realised the full implications of Our Lord's commission. It is the Holy Spirit who in the years since then has revealed and is still revealing, especially in the great Marian Shrines of Christendom (Lourdes, Fatima, Walsingham), all the implications of John being told to adopt Mary as his mother. Mary's mind at that moment was fully absorbed with the thought that she was losing her son to the grave, rather than thinking through what it meant to call John 'son'.

Up until then, Mary's whole life had been like a game of hide and seek with God. She found him in a special way when she promised to be the mother of his Son, she lost him in the Temple, she found him during those long years together at Nazareth, she lost him to his public ministry, she found him on the cross, and she lost him to the grave. Every finding and every losing was quite different from the one before. It was all part of her pilgrimage, as it is of ours too.

There was a different kind of finding in the resurrection. It is the kind which cannot be put into words, it was so amazing and so wonderful. Shortly afterwards, she experienced a new kind of losing when Jesus ascended into heaven. After that she had to be content to find him in the way in which we find him, through our prayers, through our membership of the Church, and through the sacraments, especially the Eucharist. We have a little picture of the first Christians, in the Acts of the Apostles, seated together, finding Jesus through prayer and through sacrament and Mary is there, in the middle of them, acting as a mother. She is praying for them, beginning her role as the Mother of the Church (Acts 1:12–14).

Then at last, the day came when Jesus called her, 'Come then, my love, my lovely one, come. For see, winter is past, the rains are over and gone. The flowers appear on the earth. The season of glad songs has come, the cooing of the turtledove is heard in our land' (Song of Songs 2:10–12). Mary in her death was taken body and soul into the Heavenly Places. The game of hide and seek is over. She will never lose him again, she has found him forever. Her glory is such that the last book in the Bible tells us that the glory of the sun and the moon and the stars altogether are as nothing compared with hers (Rev. 12:1). She is depicted crowned with stars and so we give her the title 'Queen of Heaven'.

What has she to say to us today? She never comes between us and Jesus. She always points us to Jesus. Her advice is the same as it was so long ago at that wedding reception in Cana of Galilee, when something had gone wrong with the catering arrangements. She beckoned one of the waiters and pointing to Jesus she said to him, 'Do what he tells you' (John 2:1–10). This is her maternal advice to us today. She prays with us and for us, like any mother for her children, and pointing to Jesus she says, 'Do what he tells you'. She knows what it means to follow this advice because she did it all her life. We are all on a pilgrimage of hide and seek as we make our way to Heaven. We are changing all the time, as our relationship with Jesus deepens and develops. Sometimes he seems very near, sometimes he seems far away, and sometimes he seems to disappear altogether. But he is always there. The darkness and the light are to him one and the same. Eventually he will call us to Heaven, as once he called Mary. Mary, our mother, will be holding our hand, Mary, whom we ask each day to pray for us now and at the hour of our death.

Mary is for everyone.

Men relate easily to her as a mother and as a woman of strong character, who followed her own line, irrespective of what others might think and say.

For women – she fulfils many of the roles of womanhood.

For the teenage girl, the unmarried woman and the nun – she is the ideal of virginity.

For the mother – she gave birth to her son, Jesus.

For the wife – she is the wife of Joseph. She takes her share in the family business of carpentry. Perhaps she kept the accounts?

For the widow – there was no Joseph to stand with her at the cross. He must have died and so Jesus handed her over to the care of John.

For the refugee – she shared that experience when she and Joseph fled to Egypt with the baby Jesus, escaping tyranny. It is a common experience for so many in today's world.

For the political woman – who can identify with some of the words of the Magnificat which have political overtones. It is important to remember that Mary and Joseph, together with their fellow Jews, lived under the domination of the Roman empire. They longed for freedom. Mary and Joseph's very inconvenient journey to Bethlehem, in the last stages of Mary's pregnancy, would not have happened if Caesar Augustus had not ordered a census to be taken,

> ... and everyone went to his own town to be registered. So Joseph set out from the town of Nazareth in Galilee and travelled up to Judaea, to the town of David called Bethlehem, since he

was of David's House and line, in order to be registered with Mary his betrothed, who was with child. (Luke 2:1–5)

The Jews resented Roman domination, with its restriction of their religious freedom and the presence in their midst of those who worshipped pagan gods. Mary was a woman of her time. When she visited her cousin Elizabeth (Luke 1:46–55) she sang the following words in the Magnificat. 'He has shown the strength of his arm, he has scattered the proud in their conceit'. Does this express the Jewish longing for the coming of a Messiah who would scatter the proud in their conceit (the arrogant Romans)? 'He has cast down the mighty from their thrones [the Romans] and has lifted up the lowly' (the Jews humble before God). 'He has filled the hungry with good things' (the Jews hungry for freedom, freedom from Roman taxation and all the other enforced restrictions of tyranny). 'And has sent the rich away empty' (the end of the displays of Roman wealth and extravagance). Mary was born and brought up in a climate of resentment of Roman oppression. She would have been aware of all the underground Jewish revolutionary movements and schemes to win back Jewish independence. Perhaps she had to think through and unravel her own hopes that her son, Jesus, might be the kind of Messiah who would win political freedom for his own people.

6

The Heart of the Matter
How to Pray the Eucharist

Now we are seeing a dim reflection in a mirror; but then we shall be seeing face to face.

(1 Cor. 13:12)

All down the centuries, since the birth of Christianity, book after book has been written about the Eucharist. There are hundreds and thousands of them, and still they pour forth from the printing presses. The Eucharist is the central act of Christian worship. It is the only act of worship which Our Lord instituted and he told us to go on repeating it until the end of time. So, Christians throughout the ages, have repeated the actions of the Last Supper. Different Christians call it by different names: Catholics usually speak of the Mass or the Eucharist; the Orthodox call it the Liturgy; Anglicans the Holy Communion Service or the Eucharist; Protestants the Lord's Supper. There are other names too but whatever name is used it always implies the repetition of Our Lord's actions at the Last Supper. The actions are the same; the beliefs differ.

The other day a Catholic said to me, 'I could not do without my daily Mass'. And I replied, 'Surely that is an unbalanced way of thinking of the Mass.' Certainly, there is a moment in the Mass when each one of us thinks of our own intimate and personal meeting with Our Lord in the act of Holy Communion. But the Mass is not a private devotion. It is something we all do together. It is a corporate act of worship. When we receive Our Lord in Holy Communion, all those present with us are receiving him too. Because of this we are all bound together, closely and intimately, not only with those receiving with us but with our fellow Catholic Christians throughout the whole world. The act of Communion binds us together with them into one corporate body. But more than that, the Mass binds us together with the whole Church and the greater part of the Church is on the other side of the grave. The Church on the other side of the experience of death is growing day by day. At the altar, at Mass, the whole Church, both in Heaven and on earth is gathered together. At Mass we meet our dear departed, we meet the angels and the saints and Our Blessed Mother Mary. We are all together, one great family. One Church, we dwell in him; One Church, above, below, though now, for the present, divided by the narrow stream of death. It is all wonderfully summed up in the words we use, 'Therefore, with Angels and Archangels and with the whole Company of Heaven . . .'. We are united with them and all our fellow members of the Church on earth, in the adoration and the wonder and the mystery of the Trinity of God and the love of God which is ceaselessly lavished upon us from the heart of the Holy Trinity. We are so overcome by the mystery, so filled with awe, that all we can do is utter those three gasps of wonder and adoration, 'Holy, holy, holy'.

The Eucharist is divided into two sections. By

that I mean God is present in the Eucharist in two different ways. In the first part we listen to God speaking to us in the reading of the Scriptures. It is the Living Voice of God speaking to us here and now. When the Gospel is read, it is the voice of Christ, not two thousand years ago, by the lake of Galilee, but in the *now* of our daily lives in the twentieth century.

After the readings the priest gives a homily, usually trying to elucidate the implications of the Scriptures for us. The homily is not a one-sided affair. It demands the co-operation of the listeners. This means they must pray that the Holy Spirit will direct the priest's words. They must be in a state of expectancy, ready and willing to receive what God is wanting to say. To listen to the homily in a destructively critical way is like seed being thrown on rocky ground. It will bear no fruit. Every homily has something to say to us if we have prayed for the right disposition. What we have heard from the Scriptures and the homily has to be taken home and mulled over during the week. So often, alas, we let the readings and the homily slip along. We are so familiar with it all. Our ears are deaf; our hearts are not receptive; our minds are all wrapped up with our own personal needs and problems; our attention is distracted. The Word of God bears no fruit.

The second part of the Eucharist repeats the

words and actions of Our Lord at the Last Supper. He took bread and wine, he blessed them, he broke the bread and he distributed both. In the Eucharist today the bread and the wine are provided by the congregation. We watch them being carried to the altar by the people, where the priest receives them. What does this gift of bread and wine from the laity symbolise? What are we thinking about as we watch it being received and placed on the altar? What does the bread symbolise? Think of its history, all the hands it has been through: the farmers sowing the seed; all those involved in the harvesting, the threshing, the reaping, the grinding into flour; the transportation workers taking the flour to the ware-houses and those packing it for sale in the supermarket and other shops; the nuns purchasing it and baking it into the small round white pieces we use at the Eucharist. So many people have earned their living producing this bread. It symbol-ises our daily work, our job, our career: all the wide variety of ways by which we earn our wage packet. In that bread is our daily toil, our daily tasks, our daily work. But unfortunately it is a blemished offering. The bread is marked with sin. So much of the work market is marred and spoilt by unemploy-ment, by unjust wages, by sweat-shop labour, by careless workmanship, by greed, theft, dishonesty and 'deals on the side'. However, flawed though it may be, our work fills a large part of our days, and as the bread is laid on the altar we each say, 'there is my week's work being offered to God'.

And what of the wine? It says in one of the psalms, 'It is wine that maketh glad the heart of man' (Ps. 104:15 AV). We associate wine with celebration, gladness and parties; we drink the health of the Queen; we toast the bride and groom. The wine is symbolic of all our pleasure and recreation. We spend our spare time in a wide variety of ways. Thousands make the world of sport their recreation. Others are never happier than when going to the theatre, to dinners, to art galleries, to balls and clubs. For others, it is walking, climbing, travelling and package holidays. Some take their recreation more quietly at home, in arts and crafts, reading and watching the television. All our recreation, celebration and the use of our spare time is taken to the altar in the wine. Again, alas, the offering is blemished. Recreation and enjoyment can be ruined by drunkenness, gluttony, extravagance and sexual promiscuity and meanness. The workaholic has no recreation to offer, only his obsession. Yet what else have we to offer to God except our daily work and our daily recreation? It is all heaped up on the altar in the bread and the wine. Unfortunately it is a messy offering because it is blemished by sin.

The incredible thing is that God accepts it. His

love is limitless and he is so happy that we want to surrender our whole lives to him by offering him our work and our pleasure, muddled amd marred though they may be by our selfishness. He receives them and transforms them. He uses them to represent in our midst today all he has done for us through the birth, the crucifixion, the resurrection and the ascension of his Son, Our Saviour Jesus Christ. The Eucharist is Christmas Day, Good Friday, Easter Day and Ascension Day all over again. All this is brought into our midst by the work of the Holy Spirit who was first sent upon us by God at Pentecost (Whitsuntide). Our blemished offering has taken on the aura of the miraculous.

On the first Christmas Day, God came down into our midst. He became one of us, hiding his glory, his power and his majesty in a newborn baby boy, whose appearance was no different from that of any other newborn baby. At the Eucharist Jesus speaks through the lips of his priest. It is Jesus who has called the priest to be his instrument. It is Jesus who once again is saying over the bread, 'This is my Body' and over the wine, 'This is my Blood'. So, once again he comes into our midst, as really and truly as on the first Christmas Day, this time hiding the glory of the Godhead, not in a baby boy but in the appearance of bread and wine which have become his Body and Blood. We need Faith. We need all the Faith which the shepherds had on the first Christmas night when they went to the manger. There was no mysterious light playing round the head of the baby or Mary his mother, such as we like to depict on paintings and Christmas cards. The baby looked ordinary, the setting was sordid. Yet, recalling their experience of the angelic host as they watched their sheep and the instruction to 'Go to Bethlehem to see the newborn boy', the shepherds made a great act of faith and, glimpsing the reality beneath the ordinary appearance, they bowed the knee in adoration. This was indeed, 'God from God, Light from Light, true God from true God'. We gaze at the Host. It has the appearance of bread. Jesus has said it is his Body and, like the shepherds, we make an act of faith and bow in adoration.

It is obvious from the words of Our Lord at the Last Supper, 'This is my body, this is my blood', that there must be some connection with Calvary, where his body was broken by the nails and his blood was poured out. What is this connection? and how can we understand it? Do we mean that at every single Eucharist Christ is physically crucified all over again? No. It could only happen once physically. 'Once, only once and once for all, his precious life he gave' (from a hymn by William Bright, 1824–1901). So, how is the crucified Christ present on the altar? It helps to think of it in this way: when a musician has written a piece of music, as he puts the last note down on the paper, it is finished, once and for all. But we can go on playing it over and over, forever bringing it alive in our midst in the here and now. So it is with the crucifixion of Jesus. It was finished, once and for all physically on the first Good Friday. In the Eucharist we play it over and over until the end of time. The crucified Jesus is in our midst and so we say that at the Eucharist we are pleading his holy sacrifice. St Paul makes this clear when he writes, 'Until the Lord comes, therefore, every time you eat this bread and drink this cup, you are proclaiming his death' (1 Cor. 11:27).

Primarily, the Eucharist proclaims the resurrection of Our Lord from the dead. There would be little use in 'playing' his crucifixion unless he had risen from the dead. If he had not risen, then the repetition of the Last Supper would be simply a memorial service for the tragic death of an innocent man and nothing more than that. It is the Risen Christ who comes to the altar. He said, 'know that I am with you always; yes, to the end of time' (Matt. 28:20), and so he is, in the Blessed Sacrament. When we receive Holy Communion, it is the Risen Lord whom we receive into our hearts. St John, in chapter 6 of his Gospel, has so much to say about the connection between the resurrection and the Eucharist: 'I am the living bread which has come down from heaven. Anyone who eats this bread will live for ever; and the bread that I shall give is my flesh, for the life of the world (v. 51), and again, 'Anyone who does eat my flesh and drink my blood has eternal life, and I shall raise him up on the last day' (v. 54). When we pray before the Reserved Sacrament in the tabernacle, aumbrey or monstrance it is the presence of the Risen Body of Christ which calls for our adoration.

And how do we think of the ascension in relation to the Eucharist? One way is to reflect on the fact that in the Eucharist God comes down to the altar and then, in the act of Holy Communion, further 'down' into our hearts. But he only comes 'down' that he may take us 'up'. At the moment of Holy Communion we ascend with him into the heart of the mystery of the Trinity of God. Every single act of Holy Communion is an ascension into the Heavenly Places, an anticipation of our future hope of life forever with God. It may not 'feel' like this. However our faith is not dependent on feelings. Faith based on feelings is a disaster.

So, at every Eucharist we are in Bethlehem, we are at Calvary, we are at the empty tomb and we are ascending into Heaven. It is all the work of the Holy Spirit, to whom we pray to come and consecrate the bread and wine into the Body and Blood of Christ. The mystery of the Eucharist is beyond all telling.

The words, 'This is my body; this is my blood', come echoing down the Christian centuries and day and night they encircle the world. They are heard on every kind of occasion: at the Nuptial Eucharist for the radiant bride and groom; at the Requiem when our coffin lies before the altar; at the ordination of every priest; behind prison bars; on board ship and in the midst of warfare. In the tiniest churches, in the mud churches of Africa and in the great and glorious cathedrals which ring the world.

What have we done to deserve such love? Every minute of the day and night the Eucharist is being celebrated somewhere. God continually pours out all he has done for us in the birth, the dying and the rising, the ascending of his Son, Jesus Christ and the descending of the Holy Spirit. It is beyond our understanding. It should fill us with a sense of great awe and wonder. A great silence surrounds the mystery. 'How silently, how silently, the wondrous gift is given' (from 'O little town of Bethlehem' by Phillip Brooks, 1835–93).

All this is beautifully expressed in a very ancient Orthodox hymn:

> Let all mortal flesh keep silence and in fear and
> trembling stand,
> Ponder nothing earthly minded, for with
> blessing in his hand,

Christ, our God to earth descendeth
Our full homage to demand.

King of kings, yet born of Mary, as of old on
    earth he stood.
Lord of lords in human vesture, in the Body and
    the Blood.
He will give to all the faithful, his own self, for
    heavenly food.

Rank on rank, the host of heaven spreads its
    vanguard on the way,
As the light of light descendeth from the realms
    of endless day.
That the powers of hell may vanish, as the
    darkness clears away.

At his feet the six winged Seraph, Cherubim
    with sleepless eye
Veil their faces to the presence as with ceaseless
    voice they cry,
Alleluia, alleluia, alleluia, Lord most high.

Liturgy of St James

7

Obstacles en Route
Difficulties in Prayer

I call all day, my God, but you never answer,
all night long I call and cannot rest.

(Ps. 22:2)

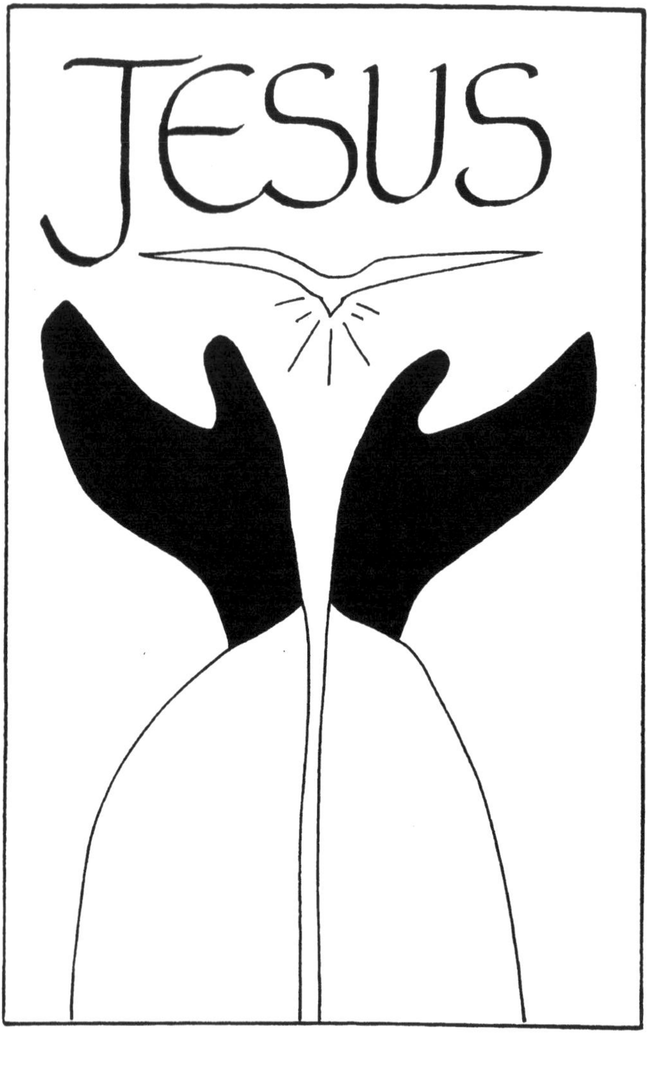
JESUS

Prayer is about making a relationship with God. It has many of the characteristics of the human relationships of love and friendship. For example, when two people are interested in each other they have a great deal of conversation at first, discovering each other's likes and dislikes. As they grow closer and love springs up they don't talk so much. They repeat short phrases, such as, 'I love you. I want you'. Finally they are happy to be together, sometimes saying nothing at all. They are so accepting of each other that they can sit in comfortable silence. It means far more than words. It is like this with God. When we begin our relationship of prayer we often do a lot of talking, using prayers from books and getting a great deal of information about God from reading the Bible, especially the New Testament. Then, as the relationship deepens we don't want to talk so much. We are happy to repeat over and over some short phrase, such as, 'O my God, I love you' or 'Jesus, have mercy on me'. Finally, words fall away and we sit in silence before God. We are 'aware' of him and the 'awareness' cannot be put into words. Silence is the sign of intimate closeness with God. These three aspects of relationship interplay. Sometimes we are drawn to one and sometimes to another.

In a good husband and wife relationship or a good friendship there must be the willingness to 'work at it'. There are always times when it seems hard, stagnant, boring and the 'grass is greener on the other side'. Forgiving each other is essential. Trying to possess the other totally for oneself is fatally destructive. Each must be given 'space' to be his or her self. Each must learn how to listen to what the other is saying. There has to be a mutual acceptance and not a constant manipulation of trying to turn the other person into what we think they ought to be. Both individuals must give time to the relationship and learn how to be together without wanting constant diversion. True close relationships are sacrificial, the constant giving, receiving, accepting and readjusting can be crucifying. All search for new life is a death to the past and this can seem frightening. We don't want to hand ourselves over. But we have to love other people for themselves and not for what we can get out of them ... There are many of the same implications for our relationship with God in prayer as in the building up of a good close human relationship. Reflect on this carefully, and your closeness to God and other persons will deepen into something very precious.

Once, someone said to me, 'Surely God knows what is best for us without us continually pestering him for it?' Yes, indeed, God does know what is best, but we are often not ready to accept it. Remember the occasion when Our Lord was on the hillside, looking down on the city of Jerusalem: the sun-washed buildings, the golden glittering dome of the Temple and the streets teeming with men, women and children. His heart went out to them all, 'O Jerusalem, Jerusalem . . . How often have I longed to gather your children, as a hen gathers her brood under her wings, and you refused' (Luke 13:34–5). How often God makes clear what he wants of us and we refuse. We cannot face the upheaval it will cause in our lives, we are set in our ways, we are frightened of taking risks. We want to be left cosy and comfortable. God never forces. We are free to choose unfulfilment.

Some people treat God like Father Christmas. They ask for a present and pull a face when it is not forthcoming! We do not think through our demands of God both for ourselves and others. We decide what we think will be best for ourselves and for others, and then demand it of him. We are really only trying to get God on our side, to give us what we want. Only God knows what is best and knowing that often means saying 'no' to our requests. When a person who is ill or in trouble seems to get worse after we have prayed for them, we get frustrated with God and shrug him off as useless. The heart of Christian prayer, both for ourselves and others, is, 'Thy will be done, not my will'. God's will may often seem very puzzling and contradictory to ours and because we are free, we can resist and resent it. We must always remember that God sees each one of our lives in its eternal perspective. If we cannot understand what he gives or allows now we shall, one day. When we take on our heavenly glorified life, it will all become clear. God's will may often seem mysterious. 'Why this?' 'Why that?', we ask as our faith in him is being tested and purified by 'fire'. Whatever trouble, anguish or sickness may afflict us, the final healing is death. Death for the Christian is no tragedy. It is a new 'flowering': the tragedy is for those left behind who mourn their loss. One of the difficult things to accept is that pain and sickness may be a privileged vocation, calling us into the heart of Christ crucified. We have all met people, disabled in one way or another, and yet they radiate 'light'. The story of St Bernadette of Lourdes makes us pause and reflect. After becoming a nun she developed cancer when she was in her mid-thirties. The other nuns said, 'You of all people must seek a cure from the water of Lourdes, you, whom God used to bring that spring of water to light.' Bernadette replied, 'I know the waters are not for me'. She died soon afterwards. Suffering is a way into the heart of God.

The Gospel portrayal of Our Lord at prayer makes a fascinating study and throws light on our wrestling with prayer. A very helpful and informative exercise would be to read through the Gospels, underlining all the passages where Jesus is at prayer. He is usually described as going away alone to pray, in the hills, across the lake of Galilee or into the wilderness. We can visualise him climbing the mountain: the sun is setting and the trees and shrubs are throwing long shadows across the grass. Our Lord is utterly worn out and exhausted. All day long he has been surrounded by demanding and often arguing people, and the merciless requests of the crowds. Our Lord, being human, is physically, emotionally and nervously drained. He climbs the mountain to get away from it all and to refresh himself by prayer and silence. Yet his whole body craves for sleep. There is nothing very easy about prayer when one is worn out.

We see him again at prayer. This time there is blood and sweat everywhere. He is in the Garden of Gethsemane on the eve of his crucifixion, struggling to accept the burden of the sins of the world and all that will entail (Matt. 26:36–46; Mark 14:32–42; Luke 22:39–46). Again and again his prayer is a cry of anguish and fear, leading to final acceptance. There is nothing soothing or consoling about that kind of prayer.

There is another description of Jesus praying as the soldiers are nailing him on the cross (Luke 23:33–4). It is a prayer of forgiveness. 'Father,

99

forgive them. They do not know what they are doing'. There is nothing glib about that kind of prayer.

Yet, we tend to think that prayer should be always easy, consoling and beautiful, no strain or stress and no difficulty. We expect God to feed us on sweets and to 'feel' his presence every time we pray. If only we would remember that, on those occasions, when we are tired and fall asleep at our prayer, shake ourselves, begin again and fall asleep again, get cross with ourselves and give up, that in fact we are very close to Our Lord, when he fought against sleep in his prayer. The very weariness is uniting us to him.

But it does not 'feel' like that.

At other times we begin to pray, full of desire for God and yet the distractions come flooding, wave after wave of them. The more we struggle against them the greater seems the onslaught. So we give up, thinking, 'What's the point?', when in fact it is our union with the distracted prayer of Christ in Gethsemane. For the 'sinless one' to accept the burden of the sins of the world past, present and to come, was a distraction we can scarce begin to fathom. Our own distraction is not coming between us and God. It is a union with and glimpse of the Christ in Gethsemane.

But it does not 'feel' like that.

And what about those times when we kneel to pray and God seems to have disappeared? The mind is a blank and all kinds of insidious doubts creep in as to whether God exists at all. 'Clouds and thick darkness' seem to lie around the very idea of God. We must not panic. It is a time of privilege, when we are being allowed a glimpse of all Our Lord endured, when from the cross he cried out, 'My God, my God, why have you forsaken me?' It is a moment of intimate union with Our Lord.

But it does not 'feel' like that.

The secret of prayer is perseverance. There will be times of light, consolation, peace and affirmation and there will be times of doubt, bewilderment, darkness and questioning. Our relationship with God is never static: it changes, develops and deepens. The day will finally come when, as we lie dying, we may feel too exhausted to pray and may even be unconscious. That will be the time when our daily life of prayer will rise up and surround us with protection and peace. Then we shall be glad that we have often prayed the Anima Christi, ' . . . in the hour of my death, call me and bid me come to you'; we shall be glad that throughout life we have kept close to the Mother of Jesus and said, 'Holy Mary, Mother of God, pray for me, now and at the hour of my death'. So, amidst all the dark and grinning faces of death, Our Lord will come to us, as once he came, walking across the storm-tossed waters of the lake of Galilee, saying, 'Peace, it is I. Be not afraid'. At last, the long years of prayer will have come to their fruition.

8

Some Scattered Leaves
Random Thoughts

'The wind blows wherever it pleases; you hear its sound, but you cannot tell where it comes from or where it is going.'

(Ps. 22:2)

Prayer is an encounter between me and God.

In any real relationship each person must be truly himself or herself. Sometimes we have a wrong idea of God which makes relationship impossible. Sometimes we don't bring to God our real selves, but only what we think he would like. We are play-acting.

We tend to present a different side of ourselves to different people. Some people enter marriage having play-acted all through courtship. We have to try to bring our real selves to God. This is not easy. How can I find out what I am like?

Give time to ask yourself, 'What was I like today when meeting this or that person? Which side of me did I present? When was I really myself? Very rarely. Some people, never. They pretend to themselves all the time. They become mad, like the woman who says, 'I am just going on holiday with the Queen' or the man who thinks he is Napoleon!

Do I find it very boring to be left to myself? Must I always have diversion? Am I too immersed in all that is happening around me? Have I grown obsessive about buying newspapers, magazines and watching the television? Who am I when all these things are taken away from me? We are frightened of getting bored when all our diversions are taken away. We feel there is nothing left. But there must be because we are made in the image of God. The discovery of our real selves is like cleaning an ancient beautiful painting which others (me) have painted over. To begin with, the more we clean the more things disappear and we begin to think we have made a mess of it, whereas before there was a certain amount of beauty, perhaps not much, but nevertheless some. However if we go on, the mess clears and the real beauty of the painting underneath (the person God created) begins to be revealed.

So we discover who we are. 'Help me, O God, to put off all pretences and to find my true self.'

The use of the Sacrament of Reconciliation helps me to discover my true self.

We have a great many mental or visual pictures of God, collected from our childhood, from the books we read or from our parents, and later from church, from priests and from other adults we meet. Quite often all these pictures prevent us from meeting the real God. They are not quite false because there is some truth in them and yet they are inadequate to the reality of God. If we wish to meet God we must make use of knowledge acquired personally or by means of hearing, listening and reading. But we must go further.

The knowledge of God which we possess today is the result of yesterday's experience. But if that is all

106

we are relying on all the time it means we are looking back and cannot meet God *now* and in the future. Of course we must let our past experience of God bring us close to him, but then we must leave the past behind, standing not before the God we know, but the God both known and unknown. What will then happen?

He may make himself known or he may give us a sense of total absence. Both are important. The experience of his absence only makes our desire for him grow stronger. We must discover ourselves and stand face to face before God, stripping off all our false images of him. It can be very disturbing.

'Help me, O God, to let go of all the false images I have of you, whatever the stress and bewilderment it brings me.'

We may feel bored and even in despair. Only when we feel totally helpless can we begin to pray.

We must never pretend with God, but tell him about ourselves just as we are. Of course he knows already, but there is a great difference between assuming that someone we love knows all about us and having the courage and real love for the person to speak truthfully and openly about ourselves.

'O God, I am tired and I don't seem able to get through to you. Why do I let my wife get on my nerves? I dig in my heels about helping with the children and yet deep down I really want to. I seem so frightened to let go of myself . . .'.

Let us lay all our worries and anxieties openly before God, leaving nothing out. Once we have done that we should drop them and leave them to him. 'Help me, O God, to let go of all my problems and fix my mind on you.'

If we don't talk openly to God about our worries and problems they will always be coming between him and us in our prayer. At every Catholic Mass we pray, 'Protect us from all anxiety'. Having got them all off our chest, what next?

There seems nothing left to say, and we feel empty and the mind is a blank. There cannot be a real meeting between two people if one of them is doing all the talking. There has to be listening too and this requires silence. We sit in the presence of the silence of God, we sit face to face with him, although we can neither see him nor feel him. We may feel at a total loss. If that is the case, say a familiar prayer (the Our Father or the Hail Mary) slowly, and reflectively.

Sometimes we get cross and feel frustrated because our prayers are not answered. That is never true. God always answers, but the answer may not be to our liking. Our Lord experienced this. In the Garden of Gethsemane as he struggled against taking on the burden of the sins of the world and the consequent betrayal, mockery, scourging and crucifixion, he cried out again and again, 'My Father, if it be possible, let this cup pass from me' (Matt. 26:36–40). God did not reply, 'Yes, of course'. He seemed to remain silent and in the silence Our Lord came to realise the answer was the very opposite to his prayer. He accepted it, 'My Father, if this cup cannot pass me by without my drinking it, your will be done'.

Many think that prayer is only real prayer if they work themselves into a great state in praying and if they manage to do this they think their prayer has power. However God cannot be 'forced' or 'bullied' and such prayer lacks all simplicity and humility.

When we gather the whole of humanity into our prayer we experience all the doubt, the anguish and the bewilderment of the human race and taste the meaninglessness which haunts so many. We see everything in its true perspective because we see it in the light of God's purpose. We carry it in silence and in patience, wondering at the privilege of sharing in the anguish of Christ for the 'lostness' of so many.

Finally, let us never forget that the obscure, dark and painful turns given to our lives are also messengers of the Invisible, except that we sometimes have to wait for eternity for them to be revealed.

ISBN 142511069-X

Printed in Great Britain
by Amazon